Please Hear Me

Lucy Jacobs

BookLeaf Publishing

India | USA | UK

Presentation by *BookLeaf Publishing*

Web: www.bookleafpub.com

E-mail: info@bookleafpub.com

ISBN: 9789358318234

First edition 2023

I would like to dedicate this book to many people.

To my children who were subject to the short fallings of schools and the Local Authority for many years but have grown up to be incredibly strong, admirable young adults

To my family who have always been there for me, despite not knowing what I was talking about half the time. Their love and support is never ending and I truly couldn't have done it without them.

To my independent support and friend; the end of our story would have been different without you, thank you.

To all the parents and carers also supporting their children with SEND: I couldn't have done it without you and now I'm here for you, you can do it, we are here for each other.

ACKNOWLEDGEMENT

Firstly, I would like to acknowledge my children for their strength and resilience against all odds.

I would also like to acknowledge our independent support and my friend, you are truly amazing. No matter how busy you are you always find the time to help others and I can't ever thank you enough for the support that you have given our family.

I also wish to acknowledge every parent and carer out there who are doing the very best they can do, don't ever let anyone make you doubt yourself.

PREFACE

This anthology of poems was written following a turbulent journey through the SEND system; a journey that the author wants to try and prevent happening to anyone else.

As a result of such a turbulent time, the author learnt much about themselves including a crucial self help tool which was the need to have time to themselves to be creative; be it writing, painting or crafts.

They also found that they needed to give back, give back for all that they had been given by others with lived and learnt experience, over the years. Something that is quite apparent in the world of SEND is the support out there from other parents and carers and the author knows that without this support, her family would not be where they are today and their children would not have the aspirations that they do.

Yes its been a rocky road and they certainly have the mental scars to show it but this story has a positive ending and it is the authors aspiration to support as many families as possible to try and achieve their happy ending.

A Letter to my Children

To my Children,

Close in age but so very different in nature,
Fierce and feisty, placid and stoic,
But both so vulnerable, small and sweet,
Both making my heart complete.

First born early, never can wait,
Second born was two weeks late!
Both with so much to give
To the big wide world where we all do live.

Watching you play,
My one wish will be
That you grow up
To thrive; happy and free.

And so my promise to you is made today,
I will support and advocate for you all the way,
I will stop what I'm doing when you need time
with me,
I won't interrupt, get distracted, I won't turn
away.

I don't promise I won't make mistakes,

Or say things that leave you in despair,
But we can work together, we can work it out,
And I will learn from this because I love and
care.

Please don't ever be scared,
Seek me out when you need.
Share your fears, hopes and dreams,
For my love is always 100% guaranteed.

Love Always
Mum xxx

I Am Me!

I
Am me.
I am me.
Not he.
Me!

It's your Responsibility

I emailed in to school last night
And asked them for some help.
A cold reply pinged straight back,
"It's your responsibility…"

I emailed in this morning,
Begging for support.
They are going to meet us at the office,
The cold response eventually replied

We stopped under the looming sign,
I hold my breath with dread.
I watch my daughter, frozen in fear,
The school's words laying heavy in my head;
"It's your responsibility"

Filled with other people's thoughts,
I try to do what's best; be firm, reassure, speak
positive.
She sighs, retracts, holds back the tears,
There's not much we can say,
I am responsible for this…

I ask if she wants me to go with her,
She says no, she's okay.

I want to pull her back with me,
I watch her walk away.

I wait until she's gone, then quickly pop inside,
Peering through the thick double doors,
I see her; back to me, alone, plodding away,
My heart breaks, no staff member to meet her,
allay her fears.

At home, catching up on paperwork,
My phone vibrates and rings,
A wave of dread passes over me
As the school number flashes on the screen.

Can I pick my daughter up?
She says she is feeling ill.
"What is wrong?" with her I ask the nurse.
"Headache and feels sick." she replies!
"Anxiety." I promptly surmise.
"You are responsible for this"

That evening, she breaks down and cries,
A cycle of despair.
Words of exhaustion, frustration and self-doubt
Come tumbling from her troubled thoughts

I listen to her muddled words,
She needs a day of rest,
A day with no overwhelm,

Where her needs can be met the best.

I call the school and tell them,
She is absent today, she is ill.
She will stay with me until she is well.
You're right, I am responsible for her!

Better Together

The gap was growing wider,
I wish I knew a way,
The SENDCo said just wait and see,
We had time, he would be okay.

I really wanted to trust them,
But time was ticking on.
I had a sinking feeling,
We couldn't wait for long!

I spoke to the SENDCo,
Assess, plan, do review;
Three terms to show the council,
for the application to get through.

My friend suggested an online SEND group,
With those that understood,
I anxiously joined and posted,
Praying that someone would.

People started replying
With news I wanted to hear!
I could request an EHC needs assessment!
The advice was very clear!

No waiting for the school,
No assess, plan, do, review,
No school waiting lists,
Or evidence building to do.

I could apply straight away,
I didn't need to wait
SEND Code of Practice Chapter nine!
The clock would start ticking from today's date!

I applied straight away
Using an IPSEA model letter.
Whatever the outcome,
I knew with my friends I would do better.

I felt so empowered,
Knew what I was doing was right,
With back up from those that knew,
The sun was shining bright.

Thank you x

The Growth of Anxiety

I wasn't born with anxiety you know,
It didn't come attached.
An incident occurred
And that anxiety it hatched.

The anxiety then grew and grew
As no one stopped to hear.
What was it that really hurt.
What made me grow in fear.

Friday Night

Most Friday evenings in our house
Are long and lacking glee
For the ping of the 5pm email
Is making its way to me.

I know that it is coming,
I know it's never good.
For I emailed them on Monday
And the reply would have been sooner if it
should!

An email we can't respond to,
That fills our heavy head,
An email set to send at five,
An email we've learnt to dread.

Across the SEND Community,
It's a day of wait and see,
The ping of the dreaded email,
Set just in time for tea.

Two long days,
Before my response is read,
Then if it isn't liked,
Back to Friday night with dread.

Please Hear Me

The girl that you see under the table;
Eyes scrunched closed, rocking and holding her
ears,
Doesn't know how to say how she feels
But hopes in her heart that someone hears.

The boy that you see throwing the pens;
Eyes scrunched closed, stamping his feet and
shouting,
Doesn't know how to say how he feels
But hopes in his heart that someone listens.

We may not always say how we feel
but see our feelings,
hear our actions,
feel our words.

The Same Jacket

The child that you see
Wearing the same jacket every day
Is a happy child,
Is a comfortable child,
Is a warm child.

The child that you see
Not wearing a jacket every day
Is a happy child,
Is a comfortable child,
Is a warm child.

The child that you see
Wearing a dirty jacket every day
Is a happy child,
Is a comfortable child,
Is a warm child.

The parent that you see
With that child every day
Is a worried parent,
Is a caring parent,
Is a loving parent.

Sensory differences you see,
Mean different for them, you and me.

Fighter

"They need to be more resilient"
"They need to just fit in."
"The world can't change for her"
"The world won't adapt for him."

These are the words
Heard from those meant to care,
Meant to understand,
But really not aware.

For resilience is shown in
Strength, persistence and standing tall,
Picking yourself up each day
When everyone around you waits for you to fall.

Resilience is never giving up
In a world that beats you down.
In speaking out loud
And in standing your ground.

So despite you standing there
Trying to change my child
Change the world around her
For this resilience may one day fold.

A Letter to my Child; I hear you

To my child,

I can see you laying there
With sadness in your eyes.
I can hear your anguish
 in your frustrated cries.

I understand you want to learn
And yearn to join in others fun
But anxiety prevents this,
Panic freezing you within.

I hear you when you tell me
that the classroom is too noisy,
And the horror that you fear
That you might get picked on.

I see your dread at the thought
 of asking for help.
Your enthusiasm for attending
now hidden behind anxiety.

I see your anger
when others give advice.

Hear your worry
when we are told you have to attend.

And I am so, so sorry
That I haven't always listened.
I am so, so sorry
That I listened to them.

But please be reassured now,
That you are not alone,
I am listening, I hear you,
in your safe place, our home.

Lots of Love always,
Mum xxx

We are Stronger Together

The friendly hum of chatter
Can be heard as you approach.
The floating aura of ease
Amongst the sea of friendly faces.

No expectation to join in,
Acceptance without judgement.
All with a common ground
Seeking support and understanding.

Lots of friendly advice,
Resources, cake and tea!
Signposting to support,
Advice for you and your family

For we are stronger together,
On common ground we run,
Sharing our experiences,
Coming together as one.

So if you haven't found us,
We are not far away,
Online or face to face,
And we really hope you stay.

Ode to the Supporter

I've known you for several years now,
As a supporter and now also a friend.
Accepting, empowering, selfless and true,
My heartful thanks to you will never end.

I remember the day you were mentioned to me,
Professional, respected, knowledgeable; it's true.
I got home and messaged you hopefully.
Instantly helping; kindness reflected in
everything you do.

Through lengthy meetings, complaints and
appeals,
Through paperwork bundles, emails and calls,
Through years of anger, hurt and tears,
Your relentless support never fails to astound
me.

And we're not the only family out there,
Who you have helped out with all things SEND.
There are hundreds of families just like us,
Who are truly grateful for that support, my
friend.

Thank you x

Listen to Our Word

Would you keep training if you didn't like
football?
Or keep attending gymnastics if you didn't like
the fall?
Could you stay still all day if you tingled in your
seat?
Or take exotic holidays if you didn't like the
heat?
Would you approach animals if you were
scared?
Or go out for the day if you weren't prepared?

Would you visit a pub if the noise was too much
to bear?
Or visit a barber if you didn't like someone
touching your hair?
Would you keep quiet of you needed to talk?
Or stay shut in a room when you needed a walk?
Would you tolerate textures that made you feel
sick?
Or eat foods that you couldn't yourself pick?

No? Neither would I!
Then why are children often expected to try?
Again and again despite upset and rage,

As an adult given freedom,
As a child, you all read from the same page.

We are all human.
We all need to be heard.
We all should have a choice.
Listen to our word!

"He will have to go without!"

A letter came home about cooking club;
An enrichment activity held during school.
"Can I go mum?" my son asked hopefully,
Followed by "It sounds really cool!"

I asked the SENDCo about support,
"He will have to go without."
"He can't" I said "That's not fair!"
"The LSA's are busy" she said without doubt.

But I knew that she was wrong,
I knew it was not fair,
My eager disabled son
Should have access the same as his peers.

For there is an Act that protects him,
Called The Equality Act 2010.
Protects disabled individuals from
discrimination.
No need for unfairness again.

No need to be forgotten,
No need to be left out,
No need to fight so hard,
The Law protects our rights...

A level playing field with others.
No disadvantage because of disability;
Reasonable Adjustments are made in anticipation,
Reasonable Adjustments made when requested.

It happened again a short while later,
When he needed a hearing aid.
"We can't pay for that!" they hastily exclaimed
"It costs too much!" They attempted to evade.

Once again, I knew they weren't being fair,
They were causing disadvantage.
So Immediately raised it with the head
And the aid was hastily purchased.

As a parent you may still wonder…
What is a reasonable adjustment?
What might be needed to help your child?
What might stand in their way?

Once they need the adjustment,
You will absolutely know,
Just what stands in the way
Of their ability to access and grow.

School policies that exclude;
Behaviour, admissions, uniform and trips.

Unlawful exclusions because of unmet needs
Excluded because of their disability.

A little more time to complete their work,
Access to fidget toys to support concentration,
Pencil grips to support motor skills,
Assistive technology to aid communication.

Quiet spaces for break and lunchtimes,
Coloured resources for reading and writing,
Frequent movement breaks to regulate emotions,
Leaving lessons early and arriving late to avoid
the busyness.

So please, if your child needs something done in
a different way,
Ask the school … please ask today.
And as long as it is reasonable,
The school must adhere without delay.

*Citizens Advice Bureau, National Autistic
Society, Scope, IPSEA.

I am that Parent

I am quiet in nature,
Mere in heart,
emotional in soul,
Shy and not making a fuss.

But as I watched my children grow
And watched the services fail
I bore an inner depth,
An inner fire to protect their soul.

A depth that I didn't know existed,
And took a long time to acknowledge.
A resilient layer of strength and persistence,
A determined wall of fire.

For I am that parent,
I will do what it takes,
To support my children
When services let them down and make
mistakes

For I am that parent,
Who will be constantly clarifying,
Because my children need me
And I will never stop trying.

For I am the parent that won't be quiet,
I say it out loud,
Challenge the system,
Stand out from the crowd.
For I love my children,
And I will ensure,
Their voices are heard,
To that I endure.

I am that parent.

Thoughts in my Head

As parents of disabled children,
We have many repetitive thoughts,
Thoughts that go round in our heads
Particularly as we lay in our beds.

As I lay awake,
In the darkness of night,
Mulling over thoughts
Of did I get it right?

"Did I spend enough time playing with my
child?"
"Did they feel neglected?" My thoughts go wild!

"Did I spend too much time chasing education?"
"And too little time with my family?"
Procrastination!

"The house is messy, but I am too tired to clean."
"The house is clean... did I spend enough time
with the children?"
I dwell on, feeling mean.

"I didn't complete therapy."
"Will my child develop? Will it be my fault!"

"The therapists will know, I'll be blamed." I
default!

"What do others think when my children don't
wear their coats?"
"Will the parents and teachers be taking notes?"

I tell myself,
"Don't worry about the above
For my children are happy
and incredibly loved."

But of course tomorrow,
When I'm lying in bed,
The same thoughts,
Will go round in my head!

Our Children, Our Future

Please don't forget,
When making your decisions,
Who is at the centre,
Of this complicated process.

Who's needs matter most.
Whose dreams are to be reached.
Who will be receiving the support.
Listen as they tell you.

Hear their voice.
For the voice of the child,
Turns to the voice of the teenager,
To the voice of the young adult.

Wanting to be heard,
Wanting to be listened to,
Wanting to help make decisions,
Wanting to make their own decisions.

Support dreams to become reality,
Support the child to become an adult,
An adult with ambition;
Guided with love and support.

Our Children, Our Future.

Help from my Friends

Over the years I've had lots of advice,
From parents and professionals who care ,
And so it's time to share with you,
A few of the best to help you prepare …

Get yourself a folder
or maybe even two!
Don't be afraid to ask for help,
we are all there for you.

Get everything in writing;
email not the phone.
You know your child more than anyone,
It's you who takes them home.

Always aim for gold;
silver is great
Don't be frightened
to stand up tall and advocate.

Others are so busy,
That your child just becomes a name,
So don't stop chasing,
Always stay ahead of the game.

Take a friend to meetings,
To take down notes.
Use meeting planners,
Make meetings matter, note down those quotes!
Look out for courses,
Workshops and webinars as well,
For the more knowledge that you gain,
The less in your head to dwell.

And not lastly, join a support group,
Online or face to face,
To help you through day to day,
A perfect offloading space.

Dear Narcissist

For too many years
You've been present in my head;
Popping up in dreams,
Filling me with dread.

Constant thoughts of times
I thought you were there to support
But when I turned to you
No response, no care, no empathy in short

You took away my confidence,
Took away my trust,
Left me with nowhere to turn
But my drive for my children still a must.

I'm not the only one you've affected
With your unfulfilling role,
Children, young people and families,
Your superiority took its toll.

But I'm taking back my headspace,
I'm taking back my life,
Because your behaviour wont dictate
Or take no more of my time.

I've learnt that I was right;
That you treated us bad.
It's taken lots of time
but I won't keep feeling sad.

And I won't let you win,
You're not taking over my life,
There are people I can trust
I need to watch my children thrive.

For we've proved you wrong
And they proved me right,
Goodbye Mr Narcissist
For I've taken back my life.

A Letter to my children;
Proud

Dear Children,

As you journey through your teens and reach
adulthood,
I cannot begin to express how proud of you I
have always been.
It has been far from easy for you but you have
conquered every hurdle;
Never looking back but planning your next
adventure.

I think back to those who did not understand,
Their words laid heavy on my heart but did not
stop you.
For you knew your own paths and developed
your own autonomy,
With us, family and supporters to guide you
through.

I am proud of the confidence you have
developed,
I am proud of your exciting aspirations.
I am proud of your bravery to take on the world,
But mostly I am proud of you for being you.

You have learnt to be who you want to be,
To wear what you want to wear,
To say no when you do not like something;
And yes when you do!

You have learnt to follow your dreams;
Even when others despair!
You have learnt to listen to your hearts,
You have learnt that you can be you.

I love and admire you both.

With lots of love

From Mum xxx

Thank you

Thank you, to those that care.
Thank you, to those who were there.
Thank you, for always listening.
Thank you, for never judging.

I will always remember
How you've supported my children,
Placed them at the centre
Of all that you did.

And the support that you gave
Will never be forgotten.
You have made a difference
To their lives and to me.

As you know,
It's been a really rocky road
But your constant warm presence
Holds a reassuring stance.

Thank you so much,
You know who you are.
Thank you so much,
You are an absolute star.